BIG BU$INE$$

Nike

Published in 2013 by Wayland
Copyright © Wayland 2013

Wayland
338 Euston Road
London NW1 3BH

Wayland Australia
Level 17/207 Kent Street
Sydney, NSW 2000

Commissioning editor: Joyce Bentley
Designer: Emma Randall
Picture researcher: Shelley Noronha

Picture Acknowledgments: The author and publisher would like to thank the following for allowing their pictures to be reproduced in this publication: cover image: Stock Connection Distribution/Alamy; 1 iStock; 4 Imaginechina Corbis; 5 Jeff Mitchell/FIFA via Getty Images; 6 Nike website; 7 ©AlamyCelebrity/Alamy; 8 Ross Dettman/AP/Press Association Image; 10 Press Association; 11 Gerry Cranham/Offside; 12 John Gress/AP/Press Association Images; 13 ASICS UK; 14 © ilian/Alamy; 15 Corbis; 16 The Granger Collection, NYC/TopFoto.co.uk; 17 The Granger Collection/TopFoto; 18 Thomas Coex/AFP/GettyImages; 19 Nike website; 20 Rich Frishman / Sports Illustrated/Getty Images; 21 Mark Peterson/Corbis; 22 George Tiedemann/Time & Life Pictures/Getty Images; 23 Nike website; 24 Thomas Coex/AFP/GettyImages; 25 Tony Bowler/Shutterstock.com; 26 Nickel/ Design Pics/Corbis; 27 © David Rogers/Getty Images for Nike. Every attempt has been made to clear copyright for this edition. Should there be any inadvertent omission please apply to the publisher for rectification.

British Library Cataloguing in Publication Data:
Sutherland, Adam.
Nike. -- (Big business)
1. Nike (Firm)--Juvenile literature. 2. Sporting goods
industry--Juvenile literature.
I. Title II. Series III. Bentley, Joyce.
338.7'68536-dc23

ISBN: 978 0 7502 8201 7

Printed in China

10 9 8 7 6 5 4 3 2 1
Wayland is a division of Hachette Children's Books, an Hachette UK company.
www.hachette.co.uk

Contents

Nike rules the world

It's July 2010, the World Cup Final between Spain and Holland. A TV audience of 715 million people (that's 10% of the population of Earth!) tune in to see the world's two best teams competing for one of the greatest prizes in sport. Both teams are wearing Nike-sponsored kits, and the scorer of the winning goal, Spain's Andres Iniesta, is wearing Nike boots.

⬆ *World champion hurdler Liu Xiang features in a Nike ad for the fast-growing Chinese market.*

Fast forward to April 2011, the Cricket World Cup Final between India and Sri Lanka. About 90% of India's 1.21 billion population watch their team lift the trophy wearing Nike cricket 'whites' (pale blue, in this case). The Indian captain and national hero, Mahendra Singh Dhoni, hits the winning runs with a Nike bat.

Just a week later, South African golfer Charl Schwartzel surges through the pack with four birdies in the final four holes to win the 2011 US Masters at the historic Augusta National golf club. Schwartzel made his charge wearing Nike clothing, and sank the winning putt with a Nike club and Nike ball. The only thing not sponsored by Nike was the winner's traditional green jacket! In every sport, in every corner of the world, top teams, and individual sportsmen and women are sporting the Nike Swoosh – on their football shirts, tennis shoes, golf clubs, even cricket bats. The brand that started life as Blue Ribbon Sports changed its name to Nike in

1978. It was the brainchild of two men, amateur runner Philip Knight and his former coach Bill Bowerman. Nike has become synonymous with the greatest values sport has to offer – teamwork, sportsmanship and above all winning! And it's Nike's association with winning, and with winners, which persuades the general public – who put on Nike products to walk the dog, jog round the park, or kick a football with their friends – to buy Nike so they can be winners, too.

At home in the USA, Nike holds a massive 45% market share, leaving competitors Adidas, Reebok and others trailing far behind. Worldwide, the brand holds an impressive 17% share of a huge $195bn (£126bn) industry.

Nike's domination didn't happen by accident, and it didn't happen cheaply. Look at every sport – from American football to mixed martial arts – and you will see dozens, if not hundreds of Nike-sponsored athletes and teams. Not to mention the expensive ad campaigns, like the groundbreaking 'Just Do It' campaign in 1988 that was chosen as one of the top five slogans of the twentieth century!

This book tells the story of Nike, from its founders' first steps in business to its current position as a retail favourite. Read on for the inside story of the sports brand that changed the world.

> **"** We wanted Nike to be the world's best sports and fitness company. Once you say that, you have a focus. You don't end up making [brogues] or sponsoring the next Rolling Stones world tour.
> **Philip Knight "**

▼ Bar chart shows Nike's growth in sales and profits since 2000.

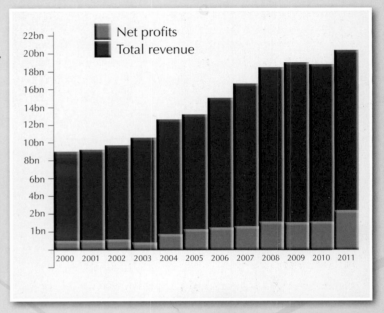

▼ Spanish footballer (and Nike wearer) Andres Iniesta scores the winning goal in the 2010 World Cup Final.

The birth of the business

Even huge, multimillion-pound businesses have to start somewhere. In Nike's case, it started with two men, a love of running, and a university project.

Philip Hampson Knight was born in Portland, Oregon in the northwest corner of the USA. An enthusiastic middle distance runner, he attended the University of Oregon, and joined the track team led by respected coach Bill Bowerman.

After graduating, Knight went to Stanford School of Business, where he wrote a project

Nike co-founder, Phil Knight in his trademark dark glasses. ▼

on launching a small business. Deciding to incorporate his passion for running, Knight thought about how he could improve the sport. Adidas made the best track shoes, but they were expensive and, at the time, hard to find in the USA. What if the Japanese could do for running what they did for cameras? Mass producing high quality and inexpensive shoes, as Nikon had done in the camera market. Knight calculated that within three years, he could be selling 20,000 pairs of running shoes per year to high school and college runners.

When his Stanford course finished in the summer of 1962, Knight set off to travel the world, and headed to Japan. In Tokyo, he discovered high quality 'Tiger' track shoes produced by a company called Onitsuka, and set off for their HQ in Kobe to meet the directors. Knight bluffed his way into a meeting, telling Onitsuka officials that he was an American importer with a company called Blue Ribbon Sports. He borrowed $37 (£23) from his father for five sample pairs of shoes from Onitsuka and headed home.

Back in Portland, Knight received his sample shoes in the post and immediately sent two pairs to his old coach Bill Bowerman, hoping for a quick sale. What he got instead was a business partner! In exchange for part of the company,

Bowerman agreed to test the shoes, get his runners to wear them, suggest design improvements, and recommend the shoes to other coaches. Knight would handle company finances and day-to-day business.

Both men put in $500 (£316) each and placed their first order for 300 pairs of shoes in February 1964. They worked out that each pair would cost them $4.06 (£2.57), and that selling them at $6.95 (£4.40) – cheaper than Adidas – would make $2.89 (£1.83) profit on each pair. Blue Ribbon Sports had gone from fantasy to reality!

↑ A modern take on the Onitsuka Tiger running shoe made for an exhibition.

Business Matters

Forming a company – a 'limited' or 'incorporated' company is a business owned by shareholders (people who own shares in the company), and run by directors. The company's shares have a basic value, for example £1 each, which stays the same, and a 'market value', which goes up and down depending on how good an investment the shares are judged to be by people outside the company who want to buy those shares.

Brains Behind The Brand

Philip H Knight – Chairman and founder

As Chairman of Nike, it is Knight's job to listen to the ideas of the board of directors, combine them with his own, and make decisions based on what's good for the company and for the shareholders. From 1968 to 1990, and from 2000 to 2004, Knight also served as company President.

It's a Chairman's job to present the company's aims and policies to shareholders, and to the outside world. He or she also leads discussions at board meetings, aiming for the agreement of fellow directors on company policy. The Chairman also plays an important role in appointing other board members.

Growing the company

Blue Ribbon was founded on a handshake between Knight and Bowerman. Once it was established, the two men were determined to turn it into a success.

When Knight first met with Onitsuka bosses in Kobe, they already had one distributor in the USA, a New Yorker named Bill Farrell who was importing Tiger wrestling shoes. At first, Farrell's involvement with Onitsuka meant the Japanese firm were reluctant to supply shoes to Blue Ribbon on a large scale. The competition made Knight and Bowerman think on their feet, however, and both men wrote to Kobe HQ to explain what a good job Blue Ribbon Sports would do with their product.

The letters worked, and Blue Ribbon received its first major order. The new company decided to target the annual Hayward Relays, the largest high school track meeting in Oregon, and Knight wrote a flyer that was included in the official information received by each coach explaining the quality of the new Japanese track shoes. However, the low price of $6.95 (£4.40) seemed to make buyers believe that the products were poorly made, and a week after the event had finished, only 31 pairs had been sold. So Knight and Bowerman targeted every track and field event they could find, selling shoes out of the back of their car, and by May 1964, Blue Ribbon was ready to restock.

Again, they faced competition from Bill Farrell in New York. This time, Knight spent the new company's first profits on a flight to Japan and managed to win exclusive rights to distribute Tiger shoes in 13 Western states. In exchange, Blue Ribbon had to guarantee orders of 5,000-8,000 pairs per year.

In 1965, Blue Ribbon hired its first salesman Jeff Johnson, another enthusiastic runner. Johnson agreed to sell the shoes part-time and was given an advance of $400 (£260) against commission on the shoes he sold. By September 1966, Johnson was selling so many shoes that Blue Ribbon owed him a further $736 (£477) in commission! It was Johnson himself who suggested it would be cheaper if he became the company's first full-time employee.

Business Matters

Retail sales — A retailer is a business that sells goods to consumers, as opposed to a wholesalers or suppliers, who normally sell their goods to other businesses. Retailers include large businesses such as Nike, with stores across the world, and also smaller, non-chain businesses run independently, such as a family-run bakery or bookshop.

It was also Johnson's idea to give away Tiger-branded T-shirts to race winners. For six months, the Tiger logo appeared on the chests of winning athletes across the Western USA. After that, the demand was so great that the company decided to start selling them.

Late in 1966, Blue Ribbon Sports opened its first retail store, on Pico Boulevard in Santa Monica, California. Started simply so that customers could try on shoes before they bought, it was the beginning of a retail operation that would stretch around the world.

▼ *University of Oregon runner Andrew Wheating (centre) poses for a photograph with Jeff Johnson (left) and his college coach, Vin Lananna (right).*

Brains Behind The Brand

Jeff Johnson – Blue Ribbon's employee
Johnson was studying anthropology (the origins of human life) at UCLA in Los Angeles when he decided he wanted to follow his passion for running. He left university and found a job as a salesman for Adidas running shoes. Then he bumped into Knight at a track meeting (the pair had once raced together) and was persuaded to sell Tiger shoes instead.

Johnson believed in the product and worked seven days a week selling them. He handled sales, orders from Japan, supplied advertisements to national running magazines and eventually ran Blue Ribbon's first retail store. Johnson and his father Owen even tried to invest in the new company but Knight refused. Instead, he got a $50 (£32) pay rise and a job opening a new store on the East Coast!

10

Better by design

Knight and Bowerman were constantly improving the design of the shoes they sold, with the aim of becoming leaders in the running shoe market.

In the late 1960s, the jogging craze hit the USA. Bill Bowerman had discovered the sport firsthand through running friends in New Zealand, and co-wrote one of the first books on the subject, *Jogging: A Physical Fitness Program for all Ages*, that sold over one million copies. Just as importantly, it made Bowerman an expert on running and running shoes in the eyes of the public.

← *Tommie Smith, US runner, trains for the 1968 Olympics in Mexico City wearing Onitsuka Tiger Cortez shoes.*

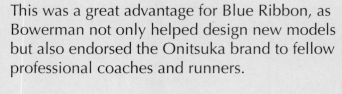

This was a great advantage for Blue Ribbon, as Bowerman not only helped design new models but also endorsed the Onitsuka brand to fellow professional coaches and runners.

At the time, German manufacturers like Adidas were making the best high-performance athletic shoes, but Knight was determined to compete with them. He asked Bowerman to design a new running shoe that incorporated the best features of several different shoes, and persuaded Onitsuka to produce them. The shoe, named the Cortez, went on sale just in time for the 1968 Olympics in Mexico City and was worn by lots of the runners. It became one of Onitsuka's best-selling shoes.

Bowerman was always trying to improve his shoe designs. Next, he suggested to Onitsuka that they should produce a lightweight running shoe with a thin layer of foam sandwiched between two sheets of nylon. The shoe would be lighter than anything on the market, which were all made of leather or canvas. Bowerman was convinced that lighter shoes would result in faster times: if he could reduce the weight of a pair of track shoes by just one ounce, a mile runner would go round the track a total of 54 pounds lighter!

The Tiger Marathon, as it became known, revolutionised the athletic shoe market. Blue Ribbon Sports signed a three-year exclusive contract with Onitsuka to sell the Marathon and their sales skyrocketed – from $86,000 (£54,000) in 1967 to $414,000 (£259,000) in 1969 and $1m (£650,000) in 1970!

US joggers hit the streets. ➤
The craze helped to sell
millions of running shoes.

Brains Behind The Brand

Bill Bowerman – Co-Founder of Nike

A successful and well-respected running coach at the University of Oregon, Bowerman was the company's head of research and development, and their first brand ambassador rolled into one. Bowerman was able to test all new products on his team of runners, improving materials, reducing weight and increasing the shoes' comfort.

As brand ambassador, he was also able to recommend the shoes to other coaches and runners he met from around the country. This growing network of constant testing and feedback also helped Nike to keep improving their shoe designs.

Business Matters

Research and development – Otherwise known as R&D, this is a business activity aimed at discovering solutions to problems or creating new goods and knowledge. Computer companies like Apple, and games companies like Nintendo use R&D to develop new ground-breaking products that they hope will be commercial successes. R&D may result in ownership of intellectual property, such as 'patents', legal ownership of new products and the technology that produced them. For example, Nike's air-cushion soles or football shirts that 'breathe' so they stay drier during a match. Nike has filed nearly 4,000 patents, while Adidas has filed just 500!

Going it alone

As the exclusive US distributor for Onitsuka's high-quality athletic shoes, Blue Ribbon was achieving $1m per year in sales. But problems existed between the two companies that threatened to destroy Blue Ribbon's business entirely.

In 1969, Phil Knight signed a new three-year exclusive deal with Onitsuka that was to run until 31 December 1972. However, Blue Ribbon was faced with several problems. Firstly, despite impressive financial turnover, the young company's profits were limited by Onitsuka's high prices. What's more, Knight often found it difficult to borrow money from his bank to meet the Japanese company's huge upfront costs of up to $300,000 (£190,000) for each new shipment.

Secondly, Onitsuka's inventory control (its ability to supply the specific shoe designs and sizes ordered by Blue Ribbon) was often erratic. Shoes arrived in the USA in the wrong sizes, the wrong colours, and often months later than expected.

This caused Blue Ribbon problems with its own clients, who threatened to boycott Knight's company – despite its high quality products – and find a distributor that could deliver the shoes it ordered, when it wanted them!

Even worse, just nine months into their new distribution deal, Phil Knight discovered that Onitsuka planned to tear up their contract and divide US distribution between up to 18 separate companies. Their reasoning was: more distributors, more sales. Under the new plans, Blue Ribbon would lose California and New York, which made up 20% of its business. It would be a devastating blow for the young company.

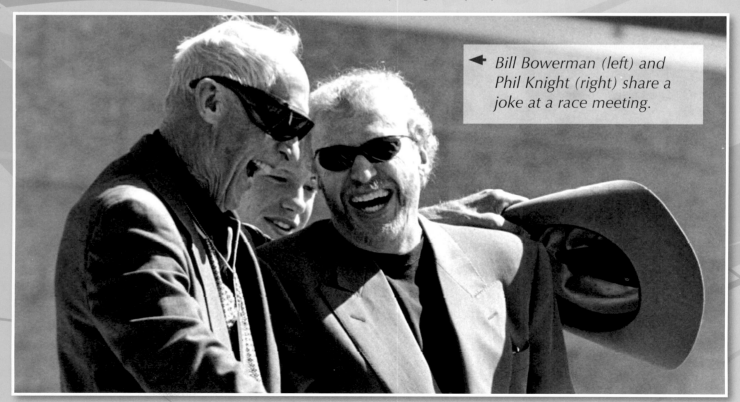

◄ *Bill Bowerman (left) and Phil Knight (right) share a joke at a race meeting.*

Onitsuka headquarters in Osaka. The Japanese company grew internationally with Knight and Bowerman's input on design.

Knight had little choice but to start looking at a Plan B. He had to risk breaking the contract himself, by finding a manufacturer who could produce Blue Ribbon's own-brand shoes, and selling them in competition to Onitsuka in the USA! He found a company in Mexico who had made shoes for Adidas for the 1968 Olympics and work was started on an American football shoe. (As Onitsuka didn't produce these shoes it wasn't a breach of their distribution contract.)

With Adidas focusing on Europe, and Onitsuka on Japan, Knight knew that there was a huge gap in the market to produce high-quality athletic shoes for the USA. He managed to secure support and funding from a US-based Japanese trade organisation whose job it was to promote Japanese products in the USA. With finance no longer a problem, Blue Ribbon was taking its first steps towards independence.

> " We originally called [the Cortez] the Aztec, because of the 1968 Olympics in Mexico City. Then Adidas threatened to sue us, as they already had a shoe called the Azteca Gold. Bill [Bowerman] said to me, 'Who's that Spaniard who [beat up] the Aztecs? Hernando Cortez.' The Cortez was born! "
>
> **Phil Knight**

Business Matters

Diversification — companies often decide to offer new products or services — like Nike expanding into football and cricket — because it reduces the risk of its other products becoming too limited or uninteresting. By adding new products to its range, Nike is providing an extra reason for users to buy their sportswear. When companies offer a completely different product or service, like supermarkets offering car or house insurance, this is called 'brandstretching'.

The Nike brand is born

Every new brand needs a memorable name and logo to help it stand out from the competition. Some companies hire marketing firms and spend years getting it right. Phil Knight sat three friends around a table and dreamed up a billion-dollar brand.

Phil Knight commissioned graphic designer Carolyn Davidson to create a shoe design as recognisable as Adidas' three parallel stripes. She came up with a large stylised 'tick' that became known as the Swoosh. None of the Blue Ribbon executives were blown away with the idea, but faced with few alternatives they gave the go-ahead to a future design classic.

Next came the search for a new name. Salesman Jeff Johnson woke up one morning with an idea fully formed in his head. Nike – what better name for a running shoe than the winged goddess of victory from Greek mythology? Davidson's Swoosh almost looked like Nike's wings and, Johnson had read, the best company names were short and contained an unusual letter like X, K or Z. Xerox, Kleenex, Zippo... and now Nike! Phil Knight wasn't convinced but said, '[Let's] go along with the Nike thing for now. I really don't like [it], but I guess that's the best of the bunch.'

In June 1971, the first Nike-branded American football shoes went on sale. However, they had been made in the warmer climate of Mexico and when they were worn in colder US winter temperatures the soles cracked in half! The 10,000 pairs Knight had ordered had to be sold at the reduced price of $7.95 (£4.95) each.

Undeterred, Knight flew to Japan to meet with independent shoe manufacturers and ordered the first Nike product line: 6,000 pairs of Tiger Cortez running shoes (now with the Nike name and Swoosh on it and renamed the Nike Cortez),

plus 10,000 pairs of tennis shoes, and assorted basketball and wrestling shoes. This was the first step to mixing sports performance and lifestyle that has been such an important part of Nike's success.

By 1973, with sales of Nike shoes on the up, Blue Ribbon finally terminated its agreement with Onitsuka. The Japanese company sued for breach of contract, and Knight counter-sued, mentioning Onitsuka's earlier plans to hire additional US distributors. After a two-year legal battle, Blue Ribbon won the right to manufacture and sell the popular Cortez running shoe with Nike branding – an important and valuable victory.

▲ *The Nike 'Swoosh', the invention of design student Carolyn Davidson, is still going strong over 40 years after it was created.*

Nikes of all sizes grace the company boardroom table at the launch of the Nike Air Force One in 1982.

Brains Behind The Brand

Carolyn Davidson – the creator of the Nike Swoosh

Davidson was a young graphic design student at Portland State University, where Phil Knight was teaching. Knight badly wanted a symbol for his new company that would become as well known as the branding on Adidas and Puma shoes, and that 'suggested movement and speed', so in 1971 he asked the designer to create a company logo.

Davidson submitted several designs, and Knight chose what became known as the 'Swoosh'. The designer was paid $35 (£22) for her time. She also became Nike's in-house designer, before leaving the company in 1983.

Business Matters

Branding — all the qualities and features of a product, including its name and its appearance, are presented to the customer as a brand. To be successful, all brands — from Nike to McDonalds to Apple — need to be distinctive (stand out in some way from competitors), consistent (always provide the same level of quality, and therefore be seen as reliable), recognisable (through a logo or 'look' of a product) and attractive. Everyone recognises Nike's Swoosh, even when they don't use the company name!

Built on innovation

One thing kept Nike shoes ahead of the competition – Bill Bowerman's obsession with finding the next great design that would give every new pair of shoes the edge in terms of performance.

Nike shoes were not just worn by athletes, they were made and sold by athletes. Bill Bowerman experimented with new materials – from nylon uppers for lighter-weight shoes, to thin foam layers for more comfort – to find the ultimate performance shoes.

In 1970, he even experimented by pouring liquid urethane (a type of rubber) onto his wife's waffle maker to try and produce a criss-cross sole that would add grip for cross-country runners racing down muddy hills, or American footballers practising on artificial turf. The waffle maker was glued shut, but a few experiments later, Bowerman had discovered Nike's familiar criss-cross waffle sole. The shoe went into production, and by 1978 was selling 100,000 pairs every month in the USA alone.

The Nike range continued to diversify – producing the first shoes designed specially for women, and unveiling improvements on older shoe models. By the end of 1972, sales had increased by 60% with 250,000 pairs of running shoes sold and, just as importantly, 50,000 pairs of basketball shoes – gaining a foothold in another important market.

Blue Ribbon sold $3.2m (£2.1m) worth of shoes in 1972, and its profits doubled each of the next 10 years. By 1978, Blue Ribbon's sales were over $36m (£23m), with $11m (£7m) in gross profit. Adidas was still the number one brand in the USA, at nearly twice the size of Converse and four times the size of Puma, with Blue Ribbon in fourth place. At this time, Knight and Bowerman decided to officially change the name of their

Nike running shoes worn by Mark Covert. Mark was the first person ever to cross a finish line wearing Nike shoes!

Nike's range of Air trainers in this 1988 ad show how the brand has concentrated on design to stay ahead of the competition.

company to Nike, Inc. By bringing the name of the product and the company together, the pair believed they could really challenge the dominance of Adidas.

Just as significantly, in 1979 the first athletic shoes with Nike air-cushioned soles were released – the Nike Tailwind. The shoe's sole was filled with tiny bags of gas – a cushioning system invented by engineer Frank Rudy (see box right) that became known as Nike Air. It allowed athletes to train harder and longer and reduced the risk of injury. It also played a major part in Nike's push to overtake Adidas as the number one athletic shoe manufacturer in the USA.

Brains Behind The Brand

Frank Rudy – the inventor of the Air sole

Frank Rudy was an ex-aerospace engineer turned inventor who created a method of trapping gas in a training shoe's soles to increase cushioning and comfort. Rudy first showed his idea to Adidas, who weren't interested, so he approached Phil Knight in 1977. Knight tried out Rudy's prototypes for himself and was amazed what a difference the cushioning made to a shoe's comfort.

Nike quickly incorporated Rudy's invention into their running shoe, the Nike Tailwind, and soon into a basketball shoe, the Nike Air Force 1. However, the Air sole really crossed over into public consciousness thanks to a 1987 ad campaign using a Beatles song 'Revolution' as its soundtrack. According to Nike President Mark Parker, '[Frank's] relentless creativity and focus on solving problems was... the template for how Nike pursues performance to this very day.'

Business Matters

Profit and loss – A profit and loss statement is a company's financial report that indicates how the revenue (money received from the sale of products and services before expenses are taken out, also known as the 'top line') is transformed into the net income (the result after all revenues and expenses have been accounted for, also known as the 'bottom line'). The document shows the revenues for a specific period, and the cost and expenses charged against those revenues. The purpose of the profit and loss statement is to show company managers and investors whether the company made or lost money during the period being reported.

Star power

From the earliest days of Blue Ribbon, Knight knew that having well-known athletes wearing and talking about your shoes was a very powerful and important endorsement for his company's sales.

In 1973, following the break with Onitsuka, Blue Ribbon were desperately searching for a way to spread the Nike name and give it some credibility with their target market – athletes. Bill Bowerman had trained a talented distance runner called Steve Prefontaine at the University of Oregon, who had just graduated and lacked the funds to keep training for the 1976 Montreal Olympics. Bowerman himself struck the deal: for $5,000 (£3,200) per year, 'Pre', as he was known, would work in the Nike store, act as liaison with other athletes, and arrange running clinics for high school and college runners.

By 1975, with sales of Nike-branded basketball shoes and boots on the increase, Blue Ribbon had signed several NBA basketball players who each received $2,000 (£1,280) per year plus a royalty from sales. By the end of the 1970s, these figures had grown to $10,000 (£6,420) per year. By 1983, around a half of all NBA players were wearing Nike shoes!

Over the years, Nike has become known for signing the biggest and best sportsmen and women – from John McEnroe and Andre Agassi in tennis, to runner Marion Jones, baseball player Derek Jeter, basketball star Michael Jordan and, more recently, golfer Rory McIlroy.

Probably the best known, and most successful, of all the company's celebrity endorsements was basketball player Michael Jordan. Signed in 1984 when he was a brand new professional, Jordan was paid $2.5m (£1.6m) over five years,

▲ *2012 French Open winner Maria Sharapova and runner-up Sara Errani, both wearing Nike.*

and had a newly-designed pair of basketball shoes, Air Jordan, named after him for which he received royalties for every single pair sold.

By 1980, the company had turned over $269m (£173m) and replaced Adidas as the most popular athletic shoe manufacturer in the US. Also in 1980, the company's growth led Knight to 'go public' with Nike, and sell shares in the company to the public.

Keen to extend their market beyond athletics, Nike also released their first range of clothing – from shorts to T-shirts – that helped to boost company growth further. By 1982, Nike had over 200 different products in the clothing line that were contributing $70m (£45m) to sales.

Business Matters

Company shareholders — shareholders at companies like Nike hope to make money in two ways. Firstly, as the company makes money, the value of its shares will rise, so an investor can make a profit if he or she sells their shares (known as a 'capital gain'). Secondly, part of the profit that a company makes every year can be given to shareholders based on how many shares they own. This is called a 'dividend'.

▼ *CEO Mark Parker is only the third man to head the global brand.*

Brains Behind The Brand

Mark Parker - President, Nike, Inc

Parker was a keen runner while at Penn State University, and joined Nike straight from college in 1979 as one of the company's first footwear designers. Over the years, he worked in a number of related areas, from product research and design, to marketing and brand management and introduced several innovations in footwear design.

By 1998, Parker had become Vice President in Global Footwear, and was named President and CEO of the company in 2001. Parker is responsible for driving the continued growth of Nike. He also oversees the company's portfolio of other businesses, including the sports and lifestyle labels Umbro and Converse, which Nike bought for $305m (£195m) in 2003.

Life at Nike HQ

Nike's World Headquarters near Beaverton, Oregon, houses over 5,000 employees and the company's state-of-the-art training and testing facilities. Welcome to the centre of the Nike universe!

Nike's World Campus, as it's know, is part-museum, part-science lab. The entrance to the 190-acre site at One Bowerman Drive, is named after the company's co-founder Bill Bowerman, and the other 18 buildings on campus are all named after famous Nike-sponsored athletes.

The largest building on campus is the 450,000 square foot Mia Hamm building. Hamm was the top goal scorer for the US Women's Soccer Team who won gold at the 1996 Olympics. The building houses Nike's product testing and development teams, and includes the Sports Research Lab, Materials and Mechanical Testing Lab and the Innovation Kitchen, where athletes' diets are devised for maximum performance.

Not surprisingly, Nike takes health and fitness very seriously, and offers free health club membership to its employees and their families. The Bo Jackson Fitness Centre is named after a famous American baseball player/footballer. It houses gyms, running tracks, weight rooms,

▼ *Nike's golf team discuss a new range of women's clothes.*

21

The Nike's HQ in Beaverton, Oregon, is a monument to the company's global success.

racquetball and tennis courts, an 11-lane swimming pool and even a 34-foot climbing wall.

On-site childcare is another benefit that Nike employees enjoy. There is a Michael Johnson running track constructed from 5,000 recycled Nike running shoes, and a Ronaldo Athletic Field (named after a famous Brazilian footballer) with two full-size football pitches.

Brains Behind The Brand

David Ayre – Vice President, Global Human Resources
As head of Nike's Global HR, Ayre's responsibilities include talent scouting great new employees, increasing their abilities through training, and then stopping them from being headhunted (hired) by other competing brands! He oversees the Nike brand, as well as other Nike-owned companies.

Ayre has over 20 years' experience in Human Resources, and joined Nike from Pepsi, where he led a bonus and benefit scheme for the company's 160,000 employees worldwide. He has a degree in economics and accounting from the University of Western Ontario and an MBA in finance from McMaster University.

Near the campus entrance, there is an international flag court, with 48 flags representing the countries where Nike did business at the time the campus was opened in 1990. The walkways between buildings form part of the Nike Walkway of Fame, with over 300 plaques commemorating the company's association with world-class athletes.

Business Matters

Human Resources — the Human Resources (HR) department of a company is responsible for putting in place and maintaining the business practices that allow effective people management. Some key responsibilities of an HR department are: 1) training; 2) staff appraisal 3) staff development: the processes in the company designed to identify the people with potential, keep them in the organisation, and move them into the right positions.

Bumps in the road

No company history is ever completely problem-free, and Nike is no exception. But facing up to problems and tackling them effectively can often make a company stronger.

From 1980-2002 (with the exception of 1987), Nike was the best-selling athletic footwear in the world. (The 'blip' in 1987 was because Nike failed to spot the growing importance of the new aerobics trend, and came second in the market behind Reebok.) By 1991, global earnings had grown to $3bn (£1.9bn), and by 1997 they were up to $9bn (£5.8bn).

Suddenly in 1998, the company hit problems. Sales dipped and, for the first time, Nike had to rethink its sales strategy and undergo a severe round of redundancies to help cut costs. Around the same time, the company also suffered a blow to its public image when it came to the attention of the press that the working conditions of overseas Nike employees in countries like Cambodia and Pakistan were substandard. Many employees were underage and underpaid, and dangerous chemicals were sometimes used in the production process.

Knight realised he had to improve Nike's image – fast! He introduced better working conditions for all workers, and slowly rebuilt the company's public image, and sales along with it. Nike now ranks among the top three in a survey of climate-friendly companies. It has also been praised for its Nike Grind programme (which recycles used trainers and uses the materials for artificial football pitches, running tracks and baseball fields).

← *An aerobics class in New Jersey, USA, in 1989. Nike failed to spot the popularity of this new sport and lost out to Reebok.*

Brains Behind The Brand

▲ *Charlie Denson is responsible for Nike's global expansion.*

For the global environmental-awareness day, Earth Day 2008, Nike launched a commercial featuring NBA star Steve Nash wearing the company's 'Trash Talk Shoe'. The shoe's upper was made entirely from pieces of leather and synthetic leather waste taken from factory floors, and the sole was composed of ground-up rubber from a shoe recycling programme. Nike claimed it was the first performance basketball shoe created from manufacturing waste.

Despite falling sales, Knight never cut back on the company's big-name endorsements. Even in 1998, Nike spent $1bn (£646m) on marketing the company. He believed – rightly – that in difficult times, the last thing that should be cut was the company's visibility!

Charlie Denson – President, Nike brand

Denson is responsible for making Nike the world's most distinctive, authentic and in-demand brand in sport. He oversees all the major sales areas: Action Sports, Basketball, Football, Men's Training, Running, Sportswear, and Women's Training, as well as the Jordan brand and Nike Golf.

Denson started his Nike career as an assistant manager at the company's first retail store in Portland, Oregon in 1979. He learned the business 'from the ground up' and understands the importance of creating and maintaining a strong connection with consumers.

Over the past 30 years, Denson has run the company's US and European operations and headed Nike's expansion into China, India and Brazil. He has been a constant innovator in developing sales and distribution strategies and driving global growth as Nike expanded into more than 160 countries.

Business Matters

Marketing – marketing is a process that attempts to understand the market and its requirements (in Nike's case, its customers and what they want from Nike products), so that the company only provides products that the market wants. Marketing creates demand with the market, thereby minimising the selling activity required. Much of Nike's success comes from celebrity endorsement – the association of the brand with winners and winning – in sports from golf to football to tennis and beyond.

A global brand

Phil Knight's vision was to turn Nike into a truly global brand. To do that, Nike had to gain visibility in the world's favourite sports – including cricket, golf and football. Just as importantly, it had to make the Nike 'buying experience' as strong in Shanghai as it was in Seattle.

Even in a 'bad' year like 1998, Nike sold 50% of all the athletic shoes in the world. International sales were mainly driven by the company's innovation in sports other than running, like football boots and 'breathable' kit – for example, the Nike Mercurial boot, worn for the first time at the 2002 World Cup.

The global audience for an event like the World Cup can have a dramatic effect on sales. During the 2010 tournament, 150,000 football shirts were sold! At the 2012 European Championships, Nike-sponsored teams included Spain, Holland and Portugal, and was worn by some of the world's greatest players.

Nike has recently renewed its sponsorship of the Indian cricket team, spending a total of $60.66m (£40m) over five years to hold off a rival bid from Adidas. This was an increase of $15m (£9.7m) on their previous five-year deal, but the sport's intense grip over the Indian public, and the potential of such a huge and growing market for other Nike products, persuaded Knight and his directors to submit a winning bid.

Nike's sponsorship of golfer Tiger Woods also opened up a world market. In 1998, when Nike launched a range of Tiger Woods shoes and clothing, the company's global golf sales rose by a staggering 80%.

▼ *Over the years, Nike has stretched its influence beyond running to hundreds of popular sports.*

↑ *The worldwide success of golfer Tiger Woods has helped Nike to gain a valuable share of the lucrative golfing market.*

Another way that Nike has extended its global reach is through its Nike Town stores. These stores usually occupy large prominent areas in cities and present Nike products in a positive way that is matched by few other brands apart from Apple.

Nike Towns sell virtually the company's entire range of running shoes and athletic clothing, and contain statues of Nike sporting heroes, giant video screens showing Nike advertising and promotional material. The first Nike Town opened in Portland, Oregon in 1990. When the Tokyo store opened, it sold $1m (£650,000) worth of merchandise in just three days! Over the past 20 years, these global superstores have provided a huge boost to Nike's visibility and revenues.

Brains Behind The Brand

Hans van Alebeek – Vice President, Global Operations & Technology

Van Alebeek is Nike's Corporate Vice President of Global Operations and Technology, which means he oversees what is known as the 'supply chain' (the process of transporting goods from factories to the stores that need them around the world). He is also head of Information Technology for the company.

Hans joined Nike in 1999 as Director of Operations for Europe after working at management consultants McKinsey & Company. In 2001, he was promoted to Vice President, Operations & Administration in Europe, the Middle East and Africa (EMEA); then Vice President, Global Operations in 2003; Vice President, Global Operations & Technology in 2004; and Corporate Vice President in November 2005.

Business Matters

Expansion — this means increasing the size of a company, or the scale of its operations. For Nike, this happened when they stopped acting as just a distributor for Onitsuka, and started to manufacture their own running shoes, and not only shoes for other sports, but also larger ranges of sports clothing. Expansion can make a business more profitable as well as more 'cost efficient', by increasing profits but keeping certain costs — like wages and office rent — the same.

What does the future hold for Nike?

For all great global businesses – from Apple to Coca-Cola – the challenge is not only getting to the top, but staying there. How will Nike continue to expand in the next ten years, and what new challenges will it face?

Probably Nike's most important challenge will be increasing its market share in fast-growing markets such as China and Russia. There are huge numbers of fashion-conscious consumers with money to spend and an eye for Western goods.

Nike currently has over 7,000 retail stores scattered across China, and Nike Brand President Charlie Denson recently confirmed that those numbers will consistently rise as Nike expands distribution to smaller cities across the country. 'The great thing about sports,' he said, 'is that it doesn't matter if you live in Shanghai,

or Beijing, or Wuhan, or wherever. You're still looking for the best and the most innovative products available, and that is what gives us such confidence.'

Nike was recently named the most powerful athletic brand in China, and business has recently started to boom. It took close to 26 years to reach $1bn (£650m) in revenue, then just four years to double it! As of May 2011, Nike generated 11.4% of its revenue from China, and that number is sure to keep growing. Nike's growing range of ACG (ALL Conditions Gear) outdoor equipment and clothing for

← The Nike brand reaches around the world. Here, two children sit in front of a hand-painted Nike sign in Mozambique, Africa.

England rugby players model their new Nike kit.

> Sometimes I look [around the Beaverton campus] and I get goose bumps [at what we've achieved]. But you better not spend much time doing that, because every six months is a new lifetime, and you've got to worry about what's coming up to stay ahead of the curve. If you spend time saying "This is cool," you're going to get your butt kicked.
>
> **Phil Knight**

sports including hiking, mountain biking and kayaking prove they will reach out to a wider range of sports fans as another way to keep sales increasing. There will also probably be a focus on more female-oriented footwear and clothing ranges for the fashion-conscious women's market.

One final area that Nike will certainly focus on is product innovation. Streamlined bodysuits have previously turned heads and shaved seconds off world record performances in running,

skating and even swimming. We are likely to see improvements in all sorts of sports equipment, from enhanced trainer performance and comfort using new and lighter materials, to golf clubs that hit the ball further, balls that fly straighter, and football boots that promise better accuracy and more power for the wearer.

One thing's for sure, Nike will continue to push the boundaries in the quest to help its athletes become world beaters. Just do it!

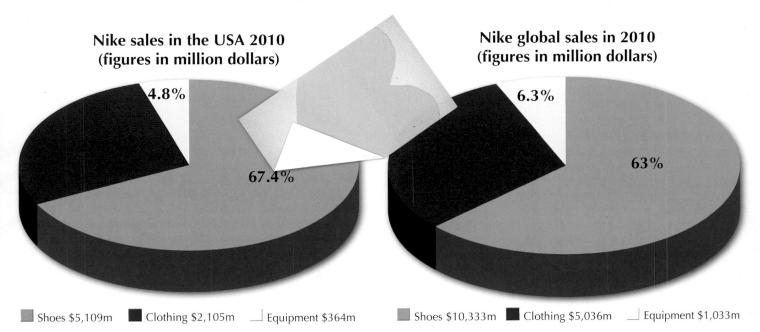

Nike sales in the USA 2010 (figures in million dollars)

4.8%
67.4%

Nike global sales in 2010 (figures in million dollars)

6.3%
63%

Shoes $5,109m   Clothing $2,105m   Equipment $364m

Shoes $10,333m   Clothing $5,036m   Equipment $1,033m

Invent the next Nike product!

To create a new product, it is helpful to produce a product development brief like the one below. This is a sample brief for a new basketball shoe called Nike Kangaroos.

The SWOT analysis on the page opposite will help you to think about the strengths, weaknesses, opportunities and threats for your product. This can help you to see how feasible and practical your idea is before you think of investing time and money in it.

Product Development Brief

Name of product: Nike Kangaroos

Type of product: New style of trainers with extra bounce. These new trainers employ Nike's new generation air cushioning system called Nike Gravity™, which helps the user jump higher and further without using any more energy. The patented shock absorption system also protects the wearer against impact injuries to feet, ankles and knees.

The product explained (use 25 words or less): This new trainer puts the air in air-cushioned soles! Jump 20% higher with our new patented 'spring' technology. Joints are cushioned and protected from injury.

Target age of users: 15-45

What does the product do? This product allows users to jump higher and further with no extra effort thanks to patented air-cushioned soles. Ultra-small gas-filled air pockets in the shoes' soles act like mini trampolines, storing the wearer's energy and then releasing it when required to push the wearer towards the skies!

Are there any similar products already available? None

What makes your product different? All good performance trainers promise bounce, comfort and support, but Nike Kangaroos will help you jump higher, further, faster - all with less effort! They will increase the performance of even average athletes, helping the user to run faster and propel themselves off the ground higher and further. Just as importantly, the shoes are designed to protect the wearer from the strains that an impact on the joints could cause.

Name of Nike product you are assessing... Nike Kangaroos (The table below will help you assess the trainers. By addressing all four areas, you can make your shoes stronger, and more likely to be a success.

Questions to consider

Does your product do something unique?

Can it be used for other sports?

What are its USPs (unique selling points)?

Strengths

Nike Kangaroos are the only basketball shoes that guarantee more bounce than its competitors.

At present, the shoe is only designed for basketball.

Why wouldn't people use this product?

Can everyone use it?

Weaknesses

Nike Kangaroos are designed for amateur players more than professionals.

Wearers need to learn how to use the shoes most effectively, and learn how to land as well as how to jump.

Can the product be improved in the future, eg adapted for other sports?

Can the product target new 'niche' (ie small, specific) markets?

Can it be used globally?

Can it develop new USPs?

Opportunities

Other versions of the shoe are being developed for track and field, for example long jump and high jump.

Joggers and distance runners may also benefit from a version of this shoe.

New versions can be developed to bounce even higher and further.

Will the shoe face competition from other products?

Is the market that you are selling in to shrinking?

Will new legislation make the shoes illegal?

Threats

Inevitably, other companies will join the market with their own version of Kangaroos.

Sports governing bodies may rule that these soles are illegal in their sports.

Do you have what it takes to work at Nike?
Try this!

1. Do you play sport?
a) Does FIFA 12 on the Xbox count? I don't play any real sports.
b) I play at school – because we have to! – but I try not to do anything in my own time.
c) Yes, I love it! I'll try my hand at anything – tennis, basketball, cross country. I love to be active.

2. Do you follow sport live or on TV?
a) I always watch Wimbledon – until Andy Murray gets knocked out.
b) I follow my local football team, plus I love watching cricket in the summer.
c) All the time! When I'm not playing sport, I'm watching it. I drive my family mad!

3. Do you know who are the World Champions or World Number Ones in a range of sports?
a) I know Spain won the last football World Cup. Does that count?
b) I have a good idea in tennis, cricket, football and Formula 1. But that's as far as I go.
c) Yep, ask me anything. I know basketball, golf, athletics, Moto GP, even badminton!

4. Have you ever thought about ways to improve the footwear or kit you use for sport?
a) Well, my tennis racket would be better if it wasn't missing some strings!
b) I try to keep up to date with the new styles of football boots – in the hope that they'll make me play better.
c) I like the idea of football boots with no laces, to give a completely smooth surface for kicking. I don't know how you would get them on, though?

5. If you had a good idea for a new product, do you think you could 'sell' it?
a) I don't have the first idea who I would even tell. Maybe my best friend?
b) I suppose I would talk to Mum and Dad and ask their advice. If they thought it was a good idea, one of us would write to a manufacturer.
c) Definitely. I've already written to Nike suggesting a way to make golf balls go straighter.

6. Do you like making plans and motivating other people?
a) Mmm, I'm not really a 'making plans and motivating others' kind of person. More like an 'extra hour in bed' kind of person!
b) I'm a little too shy to lead the way, but I'm happy to follow plans and try my hardest.
c) I always try and lead from the front – classroom rep, team captain, that sort of thing.

Results
Mostly As: Sorry, but your chances of working at Nike are looking shaky! It doesn't sound like you have the interest or the motivation to succeed in a high-pressure environment.

Mostly Bs: You are definitely interested in sports, and sporting innovation, but you need to work on your entrepreneurial skills to succeed in a very competitive business.

Mostly Cs: It definitely sounds like you have what it takes to make it to get a job at Nike! Keep working hard at school, and keep up your interest in sport, and who knows?

advance a payment made ahead of receiving money that is calculated.

birdie a score of one stroke under par on a golf hole.

brainchild an idea or invention that is dreamed up by a particular person or persons.

Brand ambassador a representative or supporter of the brand.

boycott to refuse to buy goods from someone as a punishment or protest.

calculated to work something out using maths.

company's portfolio the range of products or services offered by a company, or the list of other companies it owns.

devastating highly damaging or destructive.

distributor an agent who supplies goods to retailers.

diversify to enlarge or vary a company's range of products or the markets it operates in.

erratic unreliable.

endorsement to wear or declare your support for something.

exclusive the only person or company who has the right to sell something.

importing bringing products into a home country from abroad (often products that are not available at home).

incorporate include.

intellectual property property that is the result of creativity, such as inventions, copyrights etc.

market share the portion of a market controlled by a particular company.

NBA National Basketball Association (in the USA).

obsession an idea or thought that is constantly in someone's mind.

prototypes the first or original versions of something.

redundancies job losses.

royalty a percentage of the revenue from the sale of a product.

sponsored paid for, or contributed to the costs of something.

sporting another way of saying wearing.

state-of-the-art up-to-date, extremely advanced.

submit to show or offer something (for judgement).

surges sudden powerful forward or upward movements.

synonymous closely associated with or suggestive of something.

terminated ended, finished, closed.

turnover the total amount of sales that a company achieves (without taking off production costs, salaries etc).

ultimate the best of its kind imaginable or achievable.

visibility the prominence or importance of something.

Index